Crea
a World of
Difference

Tana Greene

Printing History
Edition One, January 2012

ISBN: 978-0-615-58230-6

Creating a World of Difference

I dedicate this book to my parents,
Buddy and Libby Bateman,
whose wisdom and unconditional love
gave me the best possible start in life.

Table of Contents

What people are saying about
Creating a World of Difference:

"If you are looking for more meaning and purpose in your life, **Creating a World of Difference** *provides a powerful blueprint. Its power comes from Tana having lived it out in her own life. Inspiring and truly helpful."*
— **Lloyd Reeb**, *Author, From Success to Significance Primary Spokesperson, Halftime*

•

"Tana Greene has created a world of difference not only in her company but also in the compelling and very human story of her life's philosophy. I was motivated to read every word and touched by her journey."
— **Marsha Firestone**, *Ph.D., President & Founder Women Presidents' Organization*

•

"(Tana's) story encourages each of us to seek our own new sense of self, whether the route is a return to school, a step up the corporate ladder or the founding of a new business. Tana made her dreams a reality. And she inspires us to do the same."
— **Mary Cantando**, *WomenBusinessOwner.com*

•

Acknowledgements

This book grew out of the eclectic paths that my life has taken and the many different individuals who have crossed my path. If it weren't for everyone I've encountered during my varied past, I wouldn't be the person I am today and I wouldn't have this story to share.

For all those experiences and for all those people, I am truly thankful. If you are reading this book, you are one of the people who has shaped my life.

Among those teachers and encouragers I include every person who has worked in my companies because they are partners in my success. I include every client who has trusted me and given me opportunities to serve them.

On my professional journey, I owe a great debt of gratitude to my colleagues in Women Presidents' Organization and to coaches, advisors and mentors like Mary Cantando and Brenda Anderson. Their insights have been rich and they have made me a stronger leader and business owner.

To my BFF Shannon, my sounding board, I can't imagine life without you in it!

I am especially thankful for my partner in life and in business, my husband Mike. He has been there with me for more than half my life now and continues to lift me daily. And to my children and grandchild, LJ, Kelly, Tracia and Keira, you bring joy to me every minute of every day. You complete me in so many ways.

                                                    - Tana Greene

What people are saying about Creating a World of Difference:

"**Creating a World of Difference** *will take you on an introspective journey that will inspire the power and awaken the spirit within you to make a difference in your business, your life and the lives of others!*"

— **Brenda F. Anderson**, *President & CEO The Galilee Agency, Inc.*

●

"*Tana Greene's book truly reveals her approach to everything she does in life. She is such a positive person and it shows in everything she does. I think every coach, teacher and mentor should read* **Creating a World of Difference.** *I loved it!*"

— **Paige Burgess**, *Ferguson Box*

Foreword

I count it as a blessing and a privilege to know Tana Greene. Tana has a wealth that goes far beyond dollars…well beyond the companies she has built, her prestigious customer lists and board positions.

The greatest wealth Tana has achieved is her giving spirit. And it is that spirit that calls her to share what she has with others—whether that be her monetary resources, her time, or, importantly as in the case of this book, her wisdom.

Tana's willingness to reach out and provide guidance and support to others is an indication that, no matter how far she's come, she remembers the experience of getting started.

Tana is magnificent—not because of what she has accumulated or even because of what she has accomplished—but because of who she has become. Through her business, Tana has experienced an epiphany, an awakening, a newfound sense of self.

Her story, in turn, encourages each of us to seek our own new sense of self, whether the route is a return to school, a step up the corporate ladder or the founding of a new business.

Tana made her dreams a reality. And she inspires us to do the same.

– *Mary Cantando*
WomenBusinessOwner.com

Each one of us helps create

the conditions that make

it possible for others to

achieve their dreams.

Each one of us helps create
the conditions that make it possible
for others to achieve their dreams.

Introduction

Have you ever headed for work and wondered if you're doing the right thing with your life? Or maybe you woke up one day and knew in your gut there had to be something more to life than making money or making ends meet. Some of us know we were meant for something more meaningful, but don't quite know what or how to change.

Creating a World of Difference is more than the name of this book. It's also more than the name of the foundation my husband, Mike, and I set up with a portion of the profits from our businesses. Creating a world of difference is the operating principle that makes our work and our lives meaningful. It is the personal standard we've set for ourselves and the professional code we've established for our companies.

For more than a decade, Mike and I believed we were in the staffing business. We were successful, too. The business grew and expanded across the country. But over time, we figured out something big:

We aren't in the staffing business filling positions;

we are in the people business, fulfilling dreams.

We were doing the right thing, but we were minimizing our contribution to the world.

Once we understood how the work we did aligned with a higher purpose, our companies started to reflect our deepest beliefs:

We believe in the power of the human spirit.

We believe everyone who desires a better life should have the opportunity to reach for that dream.

We believe each of us help create the conditions that make it possible for others to achieve their dreams.

As business owners, we've seen over and over again that if we're helping other people get where they need to be, then we'll get where we need to be. We'll be most successful when we're putting our talents and passions to work making the world a better place than it would be without our work. Dedicating ourselves and our companies to creating a world of difference has made all the difference for Mike and me, for the people who work for us, even for the businesses we serve.

Creating a World of Difference is about how we do that and why we do that – and how you can do the same, no matter what business you're in.

– Tana Greene

"How wonderful

it is that nobody

need wait a single

moment before

starting to improve

the world."

– Anne Frank

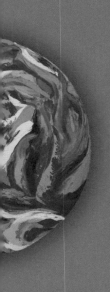

Look for the real purpose in

what you do. Look for ways

you already create

a world of difference.

Take a close look at the business you're in.
Look for the real purpose in what you do.
Look for ways you already create
a world of difference. Do more of those things.

Rebuild the Connection

Life is a series of turning points – moments when something clicks inside us and things fall into place in ways we never expected, and from that moment on, nothing is the same.

One of my turning points came a few years ago on a Sunday night when I sat in front of the TV, crying.

I feel a little silly admitting it, but this wasn't that unusual at the time. In fact, most Sunday nights you could have found me crying in front of that TV, watching, of all things, a reality show. It was one of those reality shows where a family was going through some extreme hardship like a natural disaster or a life-threatening illness. The point of the show was to interrupt that downward spiral and give that family's living space a makeover.

The family in question received a new-and-improved house, both the interior and the exterior. The people receiving the makeover always cried. I always swore to myself, "This time, I'm not going to cry."

Every time, I cried.

This particular night, I thought, What is wrong with you? This is pathetic, crying over some TV show. Is your life that empty and meaningless?

I've got to do something, I told myself. Maybe my life needs a makeover.

Soul-searching

The irony, of course, is that my life and my home certainly didn't seem to need a makeover. I had everything – a successful business, a loving family, a handsome and loving husband, my dream home on the lake. How much better could it get? I had everything anybody could possibly want.

Didn't I?

On that night, watching myself cry – again – I knew in my gut that something just wasn't right.

When my gut speaks, I listen. I learned that a long time ago, first from my father and later from the hard knocks of life itself. So I sat there on my sofa, clicked off the TV and promised myself that whatever was missing in my life, I was going to figure it out. And then I was going to change it.

That Sunday night changed not only my life, it also changed the direction of my business.

With a little bit of soul-searching, I pretty quickly realized that my life felt shallow to me. It wasn't filling me up. All I did, I told myself, was run a business. Sure, we were in the staffing business and we helped people find jobs. But it was still just...business. Making money. Selling a service. I wanted something more. I

"It is impossible

to have a great

life unless it is a

meaningful life. And

it is very difficult to

have a meaningful

life without

meaningful work."

- Jim Collins, author & business consultant

men

"Deprived of

meaningful work,

men and women

lose their reason for

existence; they go

stark, raving mad."

- *Fyodor Dostoevsky,*
Russian novelist

women

wanted to do something meaningful with my life.

I wanted to create a difference in the world.

No, it was more than that – I wanted to create a world of difference.

When the idea came to me, I felt a shiver. The tense, unpleasant feeling in my gut was gone.

Being intentional

I looked around at my wonderful life and started to worry that I was going to have to give it all up in order to do something with my life that had real value.

As it turned out, I didn't have to give up anything in order to put more meaning into my life. All I had to do was become more intentional about helping people in the ways that came naturally to me.

People who know me well would probably tell you I was born to be a people person. Like my father, I'm outgoing and positive. So sales fit me like a glove from the very beginning. Like my maternal grandmother, I'm a "fixer" – whenever someone in the family was sick, GanGaw showed up and cooked and cleaned and made sure life flowed easily until things returned to normal. I still have dreams in which my grandmother shows up to clean out my refrigerator.

I'm not big on cleaning out the fridge. But through my staffing companies I've had the chance to help a lot of people "fix" their lives by matching them with the right job, a job that would get their lives on track.

During the days when I cried over the people whose homes were getting a makeover, I had lost my connection to the real purpose of what I was doing.

Like a lot of business owners and leaders, I had let myself get into the rut of thinking it was about opening new satellite offices, or the size of the contracts, or whether our use of technology was one step ahead of the competition. Of course my life felt empty and a little meaningless.

After that night on the sofa, my husband, Mike, and I began to rededicate ourselves to the deeper purpose of our business. We began to recognize the real opportunity that comes with being successful business owners. We saw that we weren't just making money and selling a service. We weren't even just helping people find jobs. We were creating opportunities for people to have better lives. We were helping them fulfill dreams or dream bigger dreams. We were helping people take better care of their families and become contributing members of society. We were helping our client companies improve the economic circumstances of their communities.

We started telling our employees that we were in the people business. We started a foundation so we could funnel a portion of our proceeds into making life even better for associates and communities.

Through that foundation, we can help associates when a natural disaster or medical crisis stretches family resources to the breaking point. We can provide funds for training associates who want to prepare themselves for advanced opportunities. We can provide funds for organizations that our clients want to support in their communities.

When we became more intentional about living out the purpose of our business, we were making life better for others. We were doing something meaningful. Every time we filled a job, we were touching lives and creating a world of difference.

"We are all designed

for a specific purpose;

we all have something

for which each of us,

and each of us alone, is

responsible."

– Naomi Stephan, Composer

Believe the best about
others. Make sure they
know what you believe.

Believe the best about others.
Make sure they know what you believe.

② Believe in People

My first big break came in the fifth grade.

It didn't look like a big break, but sometimes that's how it happens.

I was just starting middle school in Chesapeake, Virginia. My life up until that point had looked pretty "Leave It to Beaver" normal to me – a dad I adored, a beautiful stay-at-home mom, an older brother I didn't understand, a pretty brick house in a quiet neighborhood, and church on Sundays. Middle-class perfect.

But when I was ten, something big changed.

This was the late 1960s and all over the country, schools that had been either all-white or all-black were changing. The law said they had to de-segregate. I would be bused to a school across town that had been an all-black school. My parents were outraged and frightened for us; most of my parents' friends were, too.

"We'll home school!" one of the parents said at a neighborhood meeting held in our living room right before the big change was supposed to happen.

"That's right! We can't have our children exposed to this!"

Fortunately, cooler heads prevailed. The buses came and we got on them and went to the school across town. My life suddenly expanded, in more ways than one.

The principal of the school was an African American man named Charles Brabble. I remember him as a man with a kind voice who smiled a lot and looked a lot like my father, except for the color of his skin. Looking back, I recognize that he was the first person who identified me as a leader. Maybe he was looking for a way to truly integrate some of the new white students into the life of the school. Whatever the reason, after only a few days, I was one of the children he singled out.

Mr. Brabble asked me if I would read the daily devotional over the school loudspeaker every morning. I was excited and a little nervous, but mostly it just felt right. I didn't know it then, but he saw in me the ability to speak in public, which has become a big part of my current leadership style. I now know that if we can figure out what people said about us or saw in us when we were children, we can figure out our purpose.

Later, thanks to Mr. Brabble's encouragement, I was elected school Chaplain and also received the honor of becoming President of the Principal's Committee.

I had been marked as a leader by a man I now believe was wise and perceptive and kind, a man who knew how important it was not just to this child,

"Treat people as

if they were what

they ought to be

and you help them

become what they

are capable of

becoming."

- Johann Wolfgang von Goethe,
German author

leader

"Your role as a leader

is even more important

than you might

imagine. You have the

power to help people

become winners."

- Ken Blanchard, author &
leadership expert

winners

but to the success of a noble social experiment, to bring black and white together in cooperation and mutual respect.

Planting a seed

I don't know who else Mr. Brabble impacted through his leadership during this potentially explosive moment for his school and for our country. He certainly singled me out, identified a talent no one else had pinpointed, and gave me the opportunity to use it. I doubt if I'm the only child in that school he helped in that particular way.

But I do know that Mr. Brabble created a world of difference in my life.

I called my old middle school recently, to ask about Mr. Brabble. He's still alive, still living in Chesapeake. I don't suppose he thinks of himself as a person who changed the direction of the lives of his students. He might tell you he was just a middle school principal at what was once an all-black school in the segregated South. He might tell you he did what he could to make the historic transition smooth and untraumatic for his students. He might tell you it was his job. He might tell you he just liked working with children.

Here's what I would tell you: Charles Brabble changed my life.

In reaching out and encouraging me to step into leadership roles at my new school, Mr. Brabble's actions told me that he had confidence in me. That gave me confidence in myself. He told me he trusted me, and that made me want to live up to that trust.

He told me I had certain talents I should use, and that opened my eyes to a new way to look at myself.

Just a few years after I walked into Mr. Brabble's school, I would face other challenges that took my life in unexpected directions. But Mr. Brabble had planted the seed of belief in me, a seed that grew into something I could fall back on when life turned rocky. Although many things would happen to me before I stepped into a leadership role as an adult, Mr. Brabble set the expectation that I was up to the task of leadership. I believed him. It made all the difference in my life.

Everyone has impact

In my life as a business owner, I have the opportunity every day to communicate to people that I see their talent, believe in their abilities and value their contribution. That may seem like a small thing. But it can create a world of difference in people's lives.

I could be the first person to point out a person's talents. I could be boosting someone's confidence that she can turn her life around on a day when she had given up hope. My words or actions might come at a time when someone had a critical decision to make and a nudge was all he needed to take a leap forward. It could be years before the seeds take root.

A person doesn't have to be a business owner to make that kind of impact in someone's life. Everyone has the potential to make a big difference in other people's lives. It could be the receptionist who answers the phone or the manager who sets the tone for the department or the sales person who remembers that it's all about relationships. It could be a day care worker or a bus driver...or a school principal.

Whatever role I'm in, wherever I find myself, I don't just have the opportunity to impact someone's life. I am impacting someone's life. Will it be a positive impact or a not so positive impact? If I focus on making sure it's a positive impact, I increase that chance to create a world of difference.

"Believing in people before

they have proven themselves is

the key to motivating people to

reach their potential."

- John Maxwell

Walk the

walk and

people will

follow.

Walk the walk and
people will follow.

③
Leadership by Trust

When Buddy Bateman died, the men in his church agreed about one thing: Buddy walked the walk.

John Albert "Buddy" Bateman was my father. He was my first and my biggest hero because he did the hardest thing in the world – he lived what he believed.

My dad didn't commit larger-than-life acts of heroism. I don't think he ever saved anybody's life or stopped a crime in progress. He didn't invent something that changed the world. He did serve his country in the military for two decades. He took care of his mother and his younger siblings after his parents divorced. He took care of my mother, too, because she wasn't always in the best of health.

But my dad's greatest act, I believe, was that he tried to do the right thing everywhere life took him.

Doing the right thing by the people around him was my dad's measuring stick for success, and one I try to use, too. If I can do that, I'll look up one day and realize I've changed the world for the better, one person, one day, one circumstance at a time.

Being judged for what we say or for our intentions would make life easier. But those measuring sticks have no value if what we do doesn't match up with what we're saying or what we intend. John Wooden was a legendary basketball coach; he liked to quote writer and philosopher Ralph Waldo Emerson, who said, "What you do speaks so loudly that I cannot hear what you say."

That's a problem for some people, I'm sure. In my dad's case, it worked in his favor. His actions spoke loud and clear that he was devoted to his family, his church and his community.

Parent leadership

By the time he was four years old, my dad had a nickname around the small town where he grew up. The farmers who sat around the pool hall my grandfather owned called Dad "Peanut." It started when they taught him to swear. Everytime he'd cuss for them, they gave my dad a peanut.

I guess you could say my dad's early life was short on role models.

My dad was born in Columbia, N.C., in 1925. He was the oldest of four children. In addition to the pool halls, his father owned a successful farm. When my dad was 14, his parents divorced. So at the age of 16, he joined the Merchant Marines to make money for his mother. At 18, he joined the Coast Guard. My dad felt he was the leader of his family until the day he died in 2003.

He was bedrock for the people who depended on

"Example is not

the main thing in

influencing others,

it is the only thing."

- *Albert Schweitzer*

him. And he was great with people, a natural salesman.

He also seemed to have a natural instinct for being a good father. In some ways, he was modeling great leadership – not by what he said, but by what he did. If you come down to it, a parent who can lead by example and, in doing so, teach a child what leadership looks like is giving a child a great head start in life.

The same is true in business. When we walk the walk, others will see us and know what it is to walk the walk as well.

Crossing the tracks

When I was a little girl, one of the big rules in our family was "Do not cross the railroad track."

I'm not sure why they had that rule, although I'm sure they worried that children aren't always careful about things like looking both ways at the railroad tracks. Whatever their reason, I had a better reason to cross the tracks: I liked a little boy who lived across the tracks. So I didn't always follow the rule.

One day, a train passed as I approached the tracks. I waited for it to pass, then dashed across, only to find that my mother was sitting in her car on the other side of the tracks. I was busted.

Mother then said the words that I suppose mothers everywhere used: "Wait till your father gets home."

I was relieved. Not because my dad was a softy, but because I knew he was always fair.

When Dad got home that night, he took me aside,

create

"Leaders

don't create

followers, they

create more

leaders."

- Tom Peters

leaders

"Once people can

see your spirit, they

begin to trust you. If

you are transparent,

without airs or need for

concealment, people

will be the same way

with you."

– Lou Solomon,
Say Something Real

belt in hand, and said, "Don't do that again."

And I didn't.

He didn't have to whip me. He didn't even have to raise his voice to me. Just seeing the belt in his hand told me he was serious. And because I was definitely my daddy's girl, I didn't want him to think badly of me. Getting busted again would have taken some of the shine off of my star.

But more than anything, I knew from the seriousness in his voice that this wasn't just one of those rules parents made up to keep kids from having fun. He had a good reason for telling me not to cross those tracks. And that was good enough for me because I knew what kind of man my father was.

He didn't even have to tell me his reasons to get me to follow him. I trusted him.

Culture of authenticity

When we are around others who walk the walk – who lead by example and demonstrate their beliefs through their everyday actions – it creates a world of difference in our lives. In our businesses, it creates a culture of authenticity and alignment.

That's the kind of leadership that makes a difference in people's lives. It's not leadership based on titles or ownership or org charts. It's not leadership based on fear of consequences. It's not leadership based on power.

It's leadership based on trust and confidence.

Life's hard lessons are gifts

you can use to change the

world, starting with yourself.

Life's hard lessons are gifts you can use
to change the world, starting with yourself.

④
Change Your
Own World

My life could have turned out so different.

I'm sure I'm not the only one who can say that.
Most of us have been derailed by bad decisions, poor
choices, big mistakes, even accidents or incidents we
couldn't control.

Some people say it's how we handle life's
challenges that makes the difference in how we turn
out. I believe that. But I also think it's more than just
how we handle the circumstances. I think it's what
we learn from our challenges that makes the real
difference.

Hard circumstances

I was 15 years old when my perfect, Leave-It-
to-Beaver life fell apart. The next two years were a
defining time in my life. I could write a whole book
about the two years that followed. But what I want
to focus on is how my life changed for the better
because of circumstances that could have become

a tragedy. So instead of dwelling on what happened, let me just give you the Reader's Condensed version so we can get on to what I took away from what happened.

I got pregnant. I got married. I gave birth to a son five days after I turned 16. The young man I married turned out to be physically violent. By the time I was 17 years old, I was a divorced single mother who had survived domestic violence.

It's a long way from where I was then to where I am today, the co-founder and president of an award-winning multi-million dollar national company.

I didn't get from there to here by being a victim or indulging in bitterness or blame. I got from there to here by taking responsibility for creating a world of difference for my son and myself.

That, I think, is a required step for anyone who wants to be a positive force in the world. We have to be willing to clean up the messes in our own lives before we can make a difference in somebody else's life. Not to create perfect lives, just to create lives that are authentic and reflect what we really believe and want to perpetuate.

Hard circumstances change us. It's up to us to decide if the changes will be good.

Costly diversion

My first reaction, at the age of 17, was to wonder how I could have been so blind and stupid all those years. Then I got angry and vowed to myself that nobody else was going to stand in my way. I would

"The purpose

of life is a life

of purpose."

- Robert Byrne

playing

"Life is like playing

a violin in public

and learning the

instrument as one

goes on."

- Samuel Butler

instrument

refuse to let anybody else be the reason for my success or failure. What had happened to me was not going to define me.

Somewhere I had heard about writing down goals, so I decided to set goals for what I wanted for the rest of my life. I filled a sheet of paper with those goals and a deadline for achieving them. The main goals looked like this:

- Finish school
- Buy my own house by age 23
- Get married by age 26
- Own my own business by age 30

I am sure it was that determination to define myself and create my own future that saved me from bitterness.

One by one, I set out to make all those goals become reality.

First I returned to high school because I didn't think a GED would get me where I wanted to be. Two years behind my class at that point, I managed to finish three years of high school, work part-time, take care of my son and graduate only one year behind my class. I remember it being exhausting, but I was driven.

Then, right on time, I achieved my other goals. I bought my first house at 22 and married Mike Greene when I was 26. On my twenty-ninth birthday, Mike and I signed the papers to purchase our first business, a national staffing company franchise.

I had put those two years behind me. They had been a costly diversion. But they did not throw the rest of my life into a tailspin.

Costly diversion

Those years defined me in ways I could not have expected at the time – all of them good. In fact, it's possible the difficulties that started when I was 15 were the impetus for success that has continued to drive me.

First, of course, I became a mother, which I loved even during the hardest of times.

Second, I believe that what I went through gave me compassion for other people in hard circumstances and a calling to serve people who are coming through tough times. I am motivated by a desire to give other people a way out of their own difficult circumstances because I've been in difficult circumstances myself. In addition to what Mike and I contribute by connecting people with jobs, we also operate a foundation that benefits people and communities. And I'm actively involved in fighting domestic violence in my community, especially by teaching young girls what a healthy relationship is and is not. Because of what I've been through, I have to stand up.

For me, changing my world has meant taking what could have been a tragedy and doing what I can to turn it into my gift back to the world. That's what I'm here for, to put these lessons out there, whether in a leadership role at work or in the community or with family and friends.

That's how creating a world of difference started – with realizing I could use my life lessons to make other people's lives better.

"I cannot believe that the purpose of life is to be 'happy.' I think the purpose of life is to be useful, to be responsible, to be compassionate. It is, above all, to matter and to count, to stand for something, to have made some difference that you lived at all."

— Leo C. Rosten

Money

follows passion

and boldness.

Money follows passion
and boldness.

⑤
Money Happens

My best career decisions haven't been based on money.

In fact, some of my best decisions seemed to fly in the face of financial security. If money came into the picture at all, it was more from a place of boldness or fearlessness than it was from a place of being careful.

My husband, Mike, has always been a steadying force behind the decisions that impact the flow of money. But even while he is paying attention to the money, Mike always recognizes when something is more important than money.

Calculated risk

After I finished high school, I wanted to attend a university and study art so I could teach, but I didn't have the time or the money. So I enrolled in business college and earned a secretarial certificate instead. Being disappointed or even bitter would have been easy, but that just wasn't in my nature. I had no regrets. Instead, I had this optimism that everything would work out for the best.

venturously

"If we didn't live venturously,

plucking the wild goat by the

beard, and trembling over

precipices, we should never

be depressed, I've no doubt;

but already should be faded,

fatalistic and aged."

– Virginia Woolf

precipices

My first job after completing the program at Commonwealth College was secretary to the vice president of a national motel chain. My boss was the founder's son. The thing I remember most distinctly was the corporate lobby, which was carpeted in horrible red plaid.

What mattered most about that job, though, wasn't the horrible carpet, but the fact that my boss assigned me to work directly with the ad agency that did our media buying. After about nine months, the ad agency hired me as a media buyer, where I had the chance to experience real-world applications for my love of art through commercial graphic design and typesetting. I was about 20 years old, a single mother with my own apartment, making $8,200 a year.

Then one day I got a call from Jane Braithwaite, the director of Commonwealth College – a call that changed my life in more ways than one.

A single mother herself, raising two children, Jane said, "Come see me. Get your son a McDonald's Happy Meal. I have a video he can watch while we talk."

She offered me a job recruiting for Commonwealth. "Tana, you'd make an incredible recruiter for the college. You know what it did for you. You could sell from a passionate standpoint."

I enjoyed the creative work I got to do as a media buyer, but I was drawn to the idea of helping people turn their lives around. There was one hitch. The pay was 100 percent commission. As a young single mother, the security of a steady salary – even a steady

"Don't ask yourself what the world needs; ask yourself what makes you come alive. And then go and do that. Because what the world needs is people who have come alive."

– Dr. Howard Thurman, American philosopher, author, educator and civil rights activist

salary that covered only the essentials – seemed to trump a job that spoke to my soul.

Being a single mother herself and seeing instantly why I was hesitating, Jane made a decision that changed the direction of my life. She took a calculated risk, and in doing so invited me to take one as well.

"How about this?" she said. "I'll give you a thousand a month draw against commission. At end of 30 days, we'll see how it's working out."

What the hell, I thought. What do I have to lose? I jumped at the chance.

That year, I earned $30,000 – more than triple what I would have made in the secretarial position and, in those days, a small fortune for a single mom who was barely 21.

Leap of faith

As it turned out, the passion I had for Commonwealth College did pay off, for me, for the college and for the students who enrolled there. During the six years I worked in recruiting, Commonwealth grew from an enrollment of 60 to 600. Money followed my passionate belief in the school and my deep desire to help other people succeed as I had succeeded.

I could have made $8,200 that year, if Jane had not reached out to me and taken a leap of faith on an unproven young woman.

Jane took a risk in offering me a substantial draw against money she couldn't be sure I'd earn. I took

Money followed

passion.

Money followed

boldness

 — mine and Jane's.

Money followed

trusting my gut.

a risk in walking away from a guaranteed salary for a 30-day chance to prove myself.

Money followed passion.

Money followed boldness – mine and Jane's.

Money followed trusting my gut.

The power of reaching out

More than money grew out of that experience. That day, with my son eating his Happy Meal and watching a video, my life headed in a new direction.

I could have raised my son in an apartment; instead, I was able to buy my first home in a good neighborhood where my son could grow up around other children and I could build a support network of other young mothers. I could have continued working in marketing, which I enjoyed. Instead, I realized my gift to sell. And that helped me end up where I am, doing work that helps other people in the same way Jane helped me – providing opportunities for people to launch careers, make fresh starts and find their places in the world.

That job offer created a world of difference in my life.

The most important outcome was simply that it taught me the power of reaching out to someone and trying to make a difference. A lot of my business decisions from that point on grew out of my understanding that when I had passion about something and was truly helping others, the money would follow.

When I am helping other people get where they need to be, I'll get where I need to be. Recruiting for Commonwealth College wasn't a job to me. I couldn't wait to get in there every day and show people how to do something positive with their lives.

Decades later, I'm still in the business of helping people launch careers and have more success. Mike and I own four businesses that are dedicated to placing people across the country in positions where they will thrive. We love it so much that it keeps us going, even when business is hard. Even during harsh economic times, our businesses are growing.

That's happening, I believe, because we aren't following the money. The money is following our commitment to creating a world of difference.

"I don't plan a career.

That doesn't work for me. I

just have to go with my gut."

- Ralph Fiennes, Actor

"Chase down

your passion

like it's the

last bus of

the night."

– *Poet Glade Byron Addams*

Trust

your

gut.

Trust
your gut.

⑥
Gut Instinct before Head Knowledge

The most valuable lesson my dad taught me was to think for myself.

Even as a teenager, when I had a tough decision to make, Dad never tried to tell me what to do. Instead, he would ask, "What does your gut tell you?"

I bought my first house when I was a 22-year-old single mother. I'd had my first major professional success when I took that commission-only sales job recruiting for the business college where I'd completed my nine-month secretarial course. Taking the job could have been a disaster. I could have ended up out of work with a baby to feed. Instead, I made more than three times what I'd been making at my previous job. Because of that, I felt empowered to take that grown-up step of buying a house.

Years earlier, when my first marriage had ended, I had set significant goals for myself.

The first goal was to get an education. I did attend business college, although I had wanted to get a

business

"I never get the

accountants in

before I start up a

business. It's done

on gut feeling."

- Richard Branson

feeling

four-year degree so I could teach art. But that seemed pretty much out of reach for a single mother who had to support herself and her son. Another goal was to own my own business before I was 30. A third major goal was to own my own house by the time I was 23. Thanks to my success in sales, I was a year ahead of schedule on that third goal.

Buying a first house is a big step for anyone. For a young woman on her own, it felt pretty intimidating. So I went to Dad and asked, "Am I doing the right thing?"

He said, "How does your gut feel?"

I knew the answer immediately. "Fine."

"Then you're doing the right thing."

Dad didn't just cut me loose to sink or swim. He gave me a clear measuring stick for evaluating decisions. He was telling me to pay attention to my gut. As far as I'm concerned, that's as concrete as it gets.

Just the facts, ma'am

A big part of learning to really trust your gut in business lies in the ability to do so with confidence. That's especially true for women.

For the longest time, while men were trusting their gut, women were listening to jokes about "women's intuition." We know today that it's the same thing in a different package and that women have it in abundance. But for decades – maybe centuries – we've let ourselves be talked out of trusting it. Women's intuition was cute but weak. Gut instinct was strong and reliable.

Thanks to my dad, I learned that my gut – my intuition, my instincts, my heart – knows more than my head. It never seemed to occur to him that women couldn't trust their gut just like men, so it never occurred to me, either.

No second-guessing

From the time my dad started asking me, "What's your gut telling you?" he also gave me support, no matter what my decision was or how it turned out. He trusted me to learn from my mistakes without feeling the need to make me feel guilty or stupid for them. When I was a young single mom, making bold decisions to get my life on track after already making my share of mistakes, he wasn't there second-guessing me, saying, "You can't do that."

Instead, he taught me to make decisions and be confident once I'd made them. Stick with your gut and don't waver was the example he set for decision-making. Worse than making a wrong decision was being too wishy-washy to make a decision.

I always, always knew I could count on my dad to be supportive, to be encouraging and to have my back when all else failed. From his actions, I learned to be supportive and encouraging when others are making life's tough decisions – especially if they're still learning to listen to their gut.

As a leader in business and in life, supporting others when they're learning to trust their gut isn't always easy.

"You have to

listen to what

resonates

within your own

gut. You find

your direction

there. Your voice

comes out."

- Kathy Mattea, singer

"He that gives good advice,

builds with one hand; he

that gives good counsel

and example, builds with

both; but he that gives good

admonition and bad example,

builds with one hand and

pulls down with the other."

– Francis Bacon

It's hard to leave decisions in the hands of young leaders in my business, because decisions in business almost always impact the bottom line. It's hard to give my teenage daughter the option of listening to her gut and making decisions. I know that learning to trust our gut sometimes means making mistakes.

In later years, my dad told me that the hardest day of his life was the day I sat with him and Mother and told them I was pregnant and wanted to get married. The second most gut-wrenching day, he said, was the day he walked down the aisle with me, a starry-eyed 15-year-old who had no idea what really waited behind that white picket fence she envisioned.

But as hard as it was, Dad never gave me advice. Instead, he and Mother did everything they could to back me up in the choice I'd made.

That created a world of difference in my life. If they had reacted differently, maybe I would have stayed in a bad situation longer – too long – just to prove them wrong. Maybe I would have rejected the emotional support that gave me the strength to pick myself up and start over. I don't know. I just know that their faith in me gave me a little faith in myself – and that made a world of difference at the lowest point of my life.

Eye-opener

Despite that early introduction to the importance and the validity of trusting my gut, I reached a point in life when I wasn't listening to that small still voice in me. In fact, I did everything in the world to avoid what I thought. I tried to read books, go to seminars, lead other people. Ultimately, all my avoidance led to that moment when I was sitting in front of my TV Sunday after Sunday, crying over people whose lives were undergoing transformation.

One of the things that happened for me at that point was the appearance of a mentor who really knew the mind of business owners, a man who could look at everything I was doing to deny what I knew in my gut: that I was not being true to myself.

That mentor looked me in the eye one morning and named it for me. "You have the ability to lead. You're just not allowing yourself to lead from intuition and gut."

That was the eye-opener I needed. From that point on, I remembered that Dad had been right and began once again to honor what my inner voice was telling me.

Trusting your gut doesn't always come naturally. It takes practice and self-confidence. Sometimes it takes a lot of courage and a real leap of faith. It's so easy to start listening to what others are telling you, basing decisions on emotions instead of real gut-level instinct. I had to learn all over again to stop, truly go inside and listen for that voice saying, "Wait a minute. This doesn't feel right."

When you hear that voice, trust that you have the intuition and the judgment to come up with the right solutions.

create

"It is better

to create than

to be learned;

creating is the

true essence

of life."

- *Barthold Georg Niebuhr*

essence

What's it feel like?

People ask me sometimes what I mean when I say I know something in my gut. For me, it can be as real as a burning pain when I'm about to make a wrong decision. It can be an almost sick feeling. For some people, it's that thing we call butterflies in our stomach, telling us something isn't quite right. Sometimes, it's just that small, still voice that seems to come out of nowhere, telling us what to do.

Here is one thing that is consistent: When we ignore our gut, the feeling doesn't go away. Every time we're faced with the situation that isn't quite right, we'll feel it in our gut.

When that happens, listen, especially with the big decisions. That's some higher power giving you a warning. Pay attention.

Tool for success

What does trusting your gut have to do with creating a world of difference? Here's what I believe:

- We have to be true to ourselves if we're going to fulfill our purpose. And we get true to ourselves by listening to our gut, not listening to what somebody else tells us we ought to be doing or what society or conventional wisdom say we ought to be doing.
- We will be most successful when we're listening to the directions we're getting from our gut. We have the greatest opportunity to have a positive

impact on other people when we're achieving success.

- We can teach others to listen to their gut. We do this mostly by example but also by supporting them as they learn to do it. When we do this, we're giving them one of the most important tools for success that anyone can have.

My dad taught me that. And I trusted him as much as I trust my gut.

"Creativity is a type of learning process where the teacher and pupil are located in the same individual."

- *Arthur Koestler*

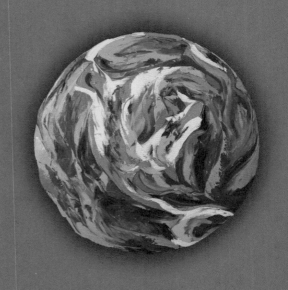

Creativity has

a bigger pay-off

than information.

Creativity has a bigger pay-off
than information.

Creativity Fuels Success

Forget Ivy League, MBAs, learning the right set of facts. That's not where it's at. Not today, when the facts learned in school are probably going to be outdated long before they get out into the real world.

Success is not about formal education – although I'm not saying education can't give you an advantage at times. I didn't get a four-year degree. But it's never held me back. That's why I can say with confidence that it doesn't matter whether you came up from the ghetto or started out with a silver spoon, whether you have an MBA or not.

More important than what you learn is to start by learning to learn. And I don't think we're teaching that in school. Not in high school, not in college, not in graduate schools. Schools teach us information.

So how do we learn to learn?

Opening my mind

I'm no expert on learning. But when I was a child, I got accolades for two things. One was my ability to stand up in front of people and speak. This became the foundation for my ability to excel as a leader and as a sales person.

The second was art, my drawings and paintings.

When I was five years old, I spent three months in bed with a serious kidney infection. I wasn't even allowed to walk to the bathroom; I had to be carried. So I only had a half-year of kindergarten. I started first grade with a disadvantage.

A bored child who wasn't even reading yet, I turned to art. I drew. I painted. I made crafts.

Maybe I wasn't learning what the other five-year-olds were learning in kindergarten. But I was learning. I was learning to be creative. I was learning to open my mind. I was learning to think in ways that didn't come strictly out of books.

So despite starting out behind my classmates in the first grade, I don't remember feeling behind. My mind had been busy the whole time I was laid up in bed. Throughout my childhood, I continued to create. I once made an entire village in our yard out of sticks and acorns.

I ignored that side of myself for a long time. I couldn't see how it contributed to making a living and taking care of my son. I know now that creativity is part of the entrepreneurial instinct that drove my husband and me to found a business that has become our platform for creating a world of difference.

In the long run, being creative had a bigger pay-off for me than the information I memorized from teachers and books.

"Authenticity is the

alignment of head, mouth,

heart, and feet – thinking,

saying, feeling, and

doing the same thing –

consistently. This builds

trust, and followers love

leaders they can trust."

- Lance Secretan

Urge to create

With a small child and a house and a job, I didn't find time in my life for art. After Mike and I married, life started moving at an even faster pace. We lived and worked in California for a few years. I was no longer feeling satisfied with going to a job and earning a paycheck. My buried creativity was starting to come out in a more entrepreneurial form.

While I was still a teenager, I'd decided I wanted to own my own business by the time I was 30. At that point, this was the only life goal I'd set that I hadn't fulfilled. I didn't know exactly what I wanted to do at that point, but I knew I wanted more independence, I knew I wanted to keep helping people…and I knew I had this urge to create something.

I started doing research in fields related to helping people with their careers. I knew the people part of the industry, but I needed to know more about the business end of things. And I wasn't afraid to learn. Within 45 days, I had done enough research to understand the opportunity in staffing. Then one day a freebie newspaper slapped into our driveway; inside was an interview with the founder of a new staffing franchise. The office happened to be a mile from our house.

When I spoke with the president of this new venture on the phone, he was stand-offish. I learned later that he had spent more than $100,000 the previous year advertising in a national publication and couldn't believe I had just walked in off the street. He thought I was a shopper.

"Be who you are and

say what you feel

because those who

mind don't matter

and those who

matter don't mind."

- *Dr. Seuss*

Mike and I purchased that company's first franchise in 1987.

By the mid-90s, we had a daughter and we were building our own company. My creative energy seemed to have plenty of good outlets.

A few years later, I found myself sitting in front of the TV, crying over episodes of "Extreme Makeover: Home Edition." Starting and building a business had satisfied my creative urges for a while, but I needed more.

Finding our creative wellspring

In addition to reconnecting with my purpose and launching the Creating a World of Difference foundation, I also returned to my art a few years ago. I struggled at first. Ideas wouldn't come. I would stare at a blank canvas and wonder why I had nothing to "say." If I tried to press on and just paint, what ended up on the canvas looked lifeless. I didn't want to give up, but I was beginning to wonder if it was just too late to pick up a passion I had discarded decades earlier.

"I can't even figure out what to paint," I told Brenda Anderson, my professional coach.

Brenda, always wise and calm, smiled and said, "That's because you're out there..." she gestured toward some undefined place "...trying to figure out what to paint. You need to go to your quiet time to discover what to paint – something that means something to you."

I had to get quiet. I had to get in touch with that creative part of myself. I had to turn off that "make it happen" mentality that's so important in business

What Our Company Believes

- We believe in ***the power of the human spirit*** to create a world of difference.

- We believe everyone who desires a better life should have the ***opportunity to reach for that dream***.

- We believe each of us ***helps create the conditions*** that make it possible for others to achieve their dreams.

and allow the creative juices to flow again. I had to recognize that creativity didn't come from training or education or strategic planning.

Eventually, I was able to paint from my true heart and spirit.

Faster track to success

Can being creative really help us create a world of difference? You bet.

First, allowing ourselves to express the talent and creativity we were born with moves us along the pathway to success faster than just earning a degree or feeding our brains with information other people have written in books. Those things are good, but when we feed our creativity, we cultivate our ability to actually learn, problem-solve and succeed.

Next, when you're creative, it releases other people to be creative, too, which multiplies the chances for success. When one person succeeds, it boosts everybody's success, from the business to the associates to clients or customers and business partners. When our businesses become places where people feel valued for their contributions, they blossom beyond what they were. They reach new levels of initiative and innovation.

I'm not the only one who sees the connection between success and creativity. The McColl Center for Visual Art, part of the legacy of former Bank of American chairman and CEO Hugh McColl, offers a six-day program designed to help corporate executives and entrepreneurs think creatively.

The program is regularly attended by engineers, physicians, marketing executives, accountants and operations executives.

Creativity fuels our success and the success of others, which multiplies the effort we've made to create a world of difference.

"Sail beyond the horizon; fly higher than you ever thought possible; magnify your existence by helping others; be kind to people and animals of all shapes and sizes; be true to what you value most; shine your light on the world; and be the person you were born to be."

- Blake Beattie

Live

your

values.

Live your
values.

You'd Better Believe It

What does your business stand for? What about your family? Does your family know the beliefs that are at the heart of your family life?

I know families who would tell you their lives are built on certain values. But their actions don't reflect those values and their family life is empty or dysfunctional or fractured.

I know business owners who think their mission statement is the end-all and be-all of their success, yet their mission statement was created as nothing more than a marketing-driven tagline. There's no heart in it and no authenticity in it and believe me, people who read it know that.

Other business people make it clear that they're in it for the money. They might call it security or taking care of their families or even providing jobs so others can take care of their families. But peel it back and they're saying their mission in life is to accumulate as much money as they can. When that's the case, life can feel pretty shallow.

The reason this happens is that the leaders in charge – owners, executives, parents, spouses – don't really know what they believe in. They haven't taken the time to dig in and find those answers. So they are not authentic in the ways they live and work.

When I can center myself around my beliefs and values, everything goes in the right direction.

Today, you could take away my house on the lake and my closet full of clothes and my car and I wouldn't feel a deep sense of loss because I no longer believe those things are core to my being and my purpose. So I've come a long way, but I'm still evolving when it comes to living out of my beliefs and values. There are still times when I don't fully accept my role as president of our company. Letting go of beliefs we learned as children isn't always easy. I was taught that women aren't supposed to lead. And I sometimes still hear my mother's voice saying I'm too bossy.

It gets easier to let go of those old beliefs when I am clear about what I do believe today. So Mike and I have taken the time to dig deep inside ourselves to find the beliefs and values that drive us. And we try every day to live those beliefs.

Some people stop at thinking about their beliefs and values. Some people take the next step and write them down and communicate them in their companies or their families. But the real test is to live them. To make sure the things we say and do, the decisions we make as company leaders, line up with

"Be the

change you

want to see in

the world."

- Ghandi

the values we've claimed for ourselves, we must:

- Name them.
- Write them down.
- Tell others about them.
- Live them.

Sometimes it's hard to name these things. We hear a lot of buzz words about beliefs and values in business and in relationships. But until I internalize and live them, until I take those internal values and impart them to all the people I come in contact with, how do I make anyone's life better?

Model, recruit, reward

How are Mike and I learning to make our beliefs and values part of the fabric of our companies?

We model it. Beliefs and values move from the top down. We know we can't set values for others unless we try to live those values. We can't write them on a piece of paper or put up posters in the break room and expect people to execute them. Either you have it internally, as leaders, or you don't. And the company will follow suit. My father taught me by example; that's the way I want to lead my organization. It's the only way to lead an authentic company.

We recruit for it. We seek to be diligent about discovering whether the values of the people we hire align with the values of our company. Not match, but align. We don't look for that alignment because we don't welcome new ideas and fresh thinking – we do! But when values align in a workplace, both the company and the individuals in the company have

ust

"If you can't

feed a hundred

people, then

just feed one."

- Mother Teresa

one

a greater chance for success. Working together 40 hours – or more – every week is intense. It's kind of like getting married; if you don't have the same values it's not going to work.

We reward it. We look for employees who embody our values of embracing diversity, innovation and service and we acknowledge them and reward them. How we do this evolves as we become more clear about our values and as we do a better job of integrating those values. We've given out a handful of awards in the history of our company, but as our company matures we expect to award many more. And it won't be a lip-service, feel-good award. Our company's awards will always say we walk the walk.

Everyday reality

The most valuable thing about letting the people who work for us know what we stand for and what we are working for is that it gives their work a significant purpose. Everyone who works within The Greene Group knows that we are not in the staffing business filling positions; we are in the people business, fulfilling dreams.

That's not a tagline or a slogan or even a mission statement. That is the reality we work in every single day.

Knowing that creates a world of difference for everyone involved with The Greene Group companies. We even have applicants for permanent positions in our companies tell us that they're applying because they read on our websites about our Creating a World of Difference philosophy. Knowing that we stand for something worthwhile excites our people and makes them feel good about showing up for work every day. They know that what they do makes a difference – not because we say it, but because we do it.

Our mission is to impact lives at every level. That creates a world of difference. If we do that with those authentic values behind it, what more do we need?

"Never work just for money or

for power. That won't save your

soul or help you sleep at night."

– Marian Wright Edelman

Everyone needs

something, sometime.

Everyone has

something to give back.

Everyone needs something, sometime.
Everyone has something to give back.

Simple Things Count

When a 15-year-old girl tells her mother she's pregnant, that mother could have a lot of reactions – and some of them might not be pretty.

To my dying day, I will never forget the conversation I had with my mom the night I gave her the news. I remember knowing I had to tell my mom and wondering how in the world I was going to be able to do it. My dad worked until 9 that night, so Mom and I were hanging out in her bedroom while I worked up the courage.

Finally, I blurted out, "You're not going to love me any more."

"Oh, yes, I will," she said.

"No," I said, looking down at my hands. "I think I'm pregnant."

Mom spoke softly and matter-of-factly. "I knew all along."

I was stunned. "How did you know?"

"You've only gotten sick every day for the last week." She reached over and hugged me. "I'm so happy to be a grandmother. I was afraid I would be too old before I got to have my own grandbaby."

I seriously doubt if Mom was thrilled with the news that she was going to be a grandmother. But that's what she chose to focus on at a time when she could see that I was in need. That might have been her finest moment. With a few simple words, Mom took away my shame and my fear. Those words and the tenderness in her voice created a world of difference for a 15-year-old who had come to her mother with a confession that had to be a parent's nightmare.

It was a simple conversation. And I believe it changed my life because of what I learned about unconditional love.

Saving grace

Mary Elizabeth Robards Bateman knew something about the need for unconditional love.

My mother was born in 1924 in Pinehurst, NC. She was the youngest of three children. When she was six weeks of age, her father was killed by a drunk driver while taking the farmhands from his tobacco farm to a ball game. He died instantly.

Her mother, Della Mae Cameron Robards, did her best to run that farm and raise those three children for the next five years. Then the Depression hit. She lost everything. And in those days, there was no safety net – no welfare, no food stamps, no government assistance of any kind.

At the suggestion of leaders in her church, my grandmother took her three children to an orphanage in Troutman, NC, so they could be fed and clothed

"Loving-kindness and compassion are the basis for wise, powerful, sometimes gentle, and sometimes fierce actions that can really make a difference – in your own life and those of others."

– *Sharon Salzberg*

fear

"Ultimately we

know deeply

that the other side

of every fear

is a freedom."

– Marilyn Ferguson

freedom

and educated while she worked at a hosiery mill in High Point, NC.

The two older children fared well at the orphanage. To this day, my uncle gets together four times a year with friends who grew up there with him. They played golf and tennis and learned to play musical instruments. But for my mother, living at the orphanage was traumatic. As long as she lived, even hearing someone talk about the comic strip Little Orphan Annie triggered her emotionally.

Mom was emotionally fragile throughout my childhood. She suffered from depression and anxiety; the medical community didn't have very effective treatments for either condition in those days. The saving grace in her life, I think, was my dad. Libby and Buddy were a good-looking couple and they were devoted to each other.

Despite everything that was going on, Mom was devoted to her family and to her church. She led the Women's Circle meetings, sang in the choir, cooked and cleaned for shut-ins in her church. She was a private person, somewhat introverted. She could cope, but she was dealing with difficult issues.

Yet when she needed to be strong, she instinctively knew what I needed and she gave it to me. And her particular experiences gave her exactly what she needed in order to respond to her own daughter's fear when the time came.

In that experience, I learned from my mother that the simplest thing can sometimes turn the tide in a person's life.

Imagine the difference

Creating a world of difference is the commitment Mike and I have made with our companies. It's a commitment we make every day, in little ways, in every area of our lives.

Creating a world of difference could be using some of your company profits to benefit a cause that is meaningful to you. It could mean giving your time to actively support that cause – I'm involved right now in raising money to build a shelter for women who need help walking away from domestic violence.

Creating a world of difference can mean matching your employee's donations to the cause of their choice. It could mean a scholarship fund for training or advanced education. It could mean spending the weekend pounding nails for Habitat for Humanity or equipping a playground in a less-than-desirable neighborhood where some of your employees work.

Creating a world of difference can be something as simple as treating the grocery store cashier with respect and friendliness. My husband, Mike, lives this every day when he is at the grocery store or the home improvement store, even in a fast food drive-thru. Wherever people are wearing nametags, he makes a point of using their names at least once. It sounds like a small thing, but it acknowledges to these people that what they do matters to someone who cares enough to call them by name.

The idea of creating a world of difference is that we each have different passions and interests and talents and skills and levels of income. But we are each given gifts to share to make the world a better place. We are each given opportunities to touch other people's lives and make them better.

Everything we do has the potential to create a world of difference for someone – even something as simple as showing acceptance and unconditional love.

Imagine how different the world would be if we all assumed that we could create a world of difference in someone's life today.

"A life of reaction is a life of slavery, intellectually and spiritually. One must fight for a life of action, not reaction."

– Rita Mae Brown

Start where

you are.

Start today.

Start where you are.
Start today.

Conclusion

It's simple, really.

Do you see any problems in your corner of the world? Do something – even if it's small – today.

Do you want to make a mark on your community? Your business? Your family? Do something – it doesn't have to be earth-shattering – today.

Do you want to leave a legacy that's bigger and more significant than the amount of money in the bank or how much your business is worth? Do something – it doesn't have to cost a fortune – today.

Then do it again tomorrow.

Imagine what a world of difference you could create if you did one small thing every day for a year. Or for the rest of your life.

Margaret Mead was a cultural anthropologist who is famous for saying, "Never doubt that a small group of thoughtful, committed citizens can change the world; indeed, it's the only thing that ever does."

I would take that a little farther: One thoughtful, committed and inspired person can create a world of difference.

That's me. And it's you.

"Story is a

medicine which

strengthens

and arights the

individual and

the community."

- *Clarissa Pinkola Estes*

Tell me what you're doing to create a world of difference. Or let me know if I can come and talk to your group, organization or company about how to create a world of difference. Contact me at TanaG@CreatingAWorldOfDifference.com. Tell me your story or let's create a world of difference together.

Summing It Up

•

Each one of us helps create the conditions
that make it possible for others to achieve
their dreams.

•

Take a close look at the business you're in.
Look for the real purpose in what you do.
Look for ways you already create a world
of difference. Do more of those things.

•

Believe the best about others —
and make sure they know
what you believe.

•

Walk the walk and
people will follow.

•

Life's hard lessons are gifts
you can use to change
the world, starting with yourself.

•

Money follows passion and boldness.

•

Trust your gut.

•

Creativity has a bigger pay-off
than information.

•

Live your values.

•

Everyone needs something, sometime.
Everyone has something to give back.

•

Start where you are.
Start today.

About Tana

Tana Greene is co-founder of a national staffing corporation that places more than 3,000 temporary employees in industries ranging from transportation, medical, scientific and light industrial.

The Greene Group, doing business as StrataForce, Road Dog Drivers and WI (Workforce Integration), operates in more than a dozen states. Greene established the first staffing entity with partner Mike Greene more than 23 years ago. Most recently, Tana has been the driving force behind establishing Creating a World of Difference, a foundation that sets aside a portion of The Greene Group's corporate profits to benefit employees of client companies. The Greene Group is headquartered in Davidson, NC.

Honors and recognitions include:

- 2010 – Finalist, *The Charlotte Business Journal's* Best Places to Work
- 2009 – Named by *The Mecklenburg Times* one of Charlotte's Most Influential Women
- 2008 and 2007 – *INC Magazine's Top 5000* fastest growing national companies
- 2006 – *Enterprising Women magazine*, Enterprising Woman of the Year
- 2005 – *The Charlotte Business Journal*, Women in Business award winner
- 2005 – *Charlotte Chamber of Commerce*, Trailblazer Award

In addition to growing her own corporation, Tana is an active member of Women Presidents' Organization and serves on boards for the Charlotte Chamber of Commerce, United Family Services and The Employers Association. She advocates on behalf of victims of domestic violence, including serving on the Steering Committee to raise money for a new women's shelter in Charlotte and as Keynote Speaker for the Avon Walk to raise awareness of the issue of domestic violence.

Tana lives in the Charlotte area with her husband and business partner, Mike Greene, and their daughter, Kelly. Tana's son, L.J., his wife and their baby also live in the area.

Creating a World of Difference

Painted and created by Tana Greene.

It took me 4 months and 2 hours to create this work of art. Four months to think about the many complex things I wanted, needed and "had" to create and include, four months of trials and procrastination to work towards this hope for a perfect masterpiece. Then, once I decided I was making this way more complicated than it needed to be...I got out of my own way, removed my own fears then I let it flow...in two hours it became perfect in its own way... from my heart through my hand and to you...enjoy.

"If you find it

in your heart

to care for

somebody else,

you will have

succeeded."

– *Maya Angelou*

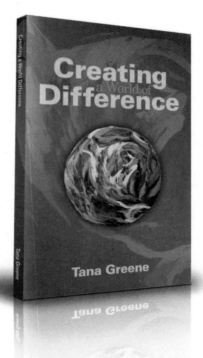

To order additional copies,
leave comments or learn
more about the Creating
a World of Difference
Foundation, go to:

www.**CreatingAWorldOfDifference**.com